The Natural World

ANTARCTICA

Steve Goldsworthy

MEDIA ENHANCED BOOKS
AV2 BY WEIGL™
ADDED VALUE • AUDIO VISUAL

www.av2books.com

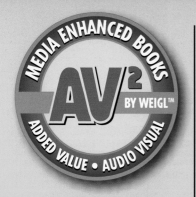

AV² provides enriched content that supplements and complements this book
Weigl's AV² books strive to create inspired learning and engage young mind
in a total learning experience.

Your AV² Media Enhanced books come alive with...

Audio
Listen to sections of
the book read aloud.

Key Words
Study vocabulary, and
complete a matching
word activity.

Video
Watch informative
video clips.

Quizzes
Test your knowledge.

Embedded Weblinks
Gain additional information
for research.

Slide Show
View images and
captions, and prepare
a presentation.

Try This!
Complete activities and
hands-on experiments.

... and much, much more!

Go to **www.av2books.com**,
and enter this book's
unique code.

BOOK CODE

G 7 5 2 6 7

AV² by Weigl brings you media
enhanced books that support
active learning.

Published by AV² by Weigl
350 5th Avenue, 59th Floor
New York, NY 10118
Websites: www.av2books.com www.weigl.com

Library of Congress Cataloging-in-Publication Data

Goldsworthy, Steve, author.
Antarctica / Steve Goldsworthy.
pages cm. -- (The natural world)
Summary: "Antarctica covers almost 20 percent of the Southern Hemisphere. Its landscape is dominated by the world's largest ice sheet. Learn more about this
exciting environment in Antarctica. This is an AV2 media enhanced book. A unique book code printed on page 2 unlocks multimedia content. This book comes
alive with video, audio, weblinks, slide shows, activities, hands-on experiments, and much more."-- Provided by publisher.
Includes index.
ISBN 978-1-4896-0938-0 (hardcover : alk. paper) -- ISBN 978-1-4896-0939-7 (softcover : alk. paper) --
ISBN 978-1-4896-0940-3 (single user ebk.) -- ISBN 978-1-4896-0941-0 (multi user ebk.)
1. Natural history--Antarctica--Juvenile literature. 2. Ecology--Antarctica--Juvenile literature. 3. Antarctica--Environmental conditions--Juvenile literature. I.
Title.
QH541.5.P6G65 2015
578.09989--dc23
2014004670

Printed in the United States of America in Brainerd, Minnesota
2 3 4 5 6 7 8 9 0 19 18 17 16 15

092015
WEP080915

Editor: Heather Kissock
Design: Mandy Christiansen

Every reasonable effort has been made to trace ownership and to obtain
permission to reprint copyright material. The publishers would be pleased to
have any errors or omissions brought to their attention so that they may be
corrected in subsequent printings.

Weigl acknowledges Getty Images as its primary image supplier for this title.
Page 14L: Nature's Pic Images.

Contents

Welcome to Antarctica!

Antarctica is the fifth largest continent in the world. It is larger than Australia and Europe. This ice-covered continent has an area that is almost 5.5 million square miles (14.2 million square kilometers). The Antarctic ice sheet, the world's largest ice sheet, towers above the landscape. It covers 5.29 million square miles (13.7 million sq. km). This leaves only 108,110 square miles (280,000 sq. km) free of ice.

Antarctica is the coldest and driest continent on Earth. Despite these harsh conditions, Antarctica is home to plant and animal life. Plant life includes almost 100 **species** of mosses and nearly 400 species of lichens. There are 200 Antarctic fish species and several species of whales and seals that live near shorelines. Large numbers of insects and microscopic animals are also found on the continent.

16,050 feet
The height of Antarctica's highest mountain, Vinson Massif (4,892 meters).

A thick ice sheet covers
98%
of Antarctica.
Only 2% is barren rock.

90% of the ice found on Earth is found in Antarctica.

If the Antarctic ice sheet melted, the world's oceans would rise by 200 feet (60 m).

The emperor penguin is the only animal to spend the long winter on Antarctica's open ice.

Unique Antarctic Life

Antarctica's ecosystems are unique because the plant and animal life adapt to extreme conditions. There are a number of species only found on this frozen continent. Birds such as the emperor penguin are called **endemic** species because they live exclusively on Antarctica.

Many plants could not survive the extremely dry conditions on Antarctica. Lichens are slow growing and thrive in severe cold. They do not require much water to live.

Animals that adapt to extreme conditions are called extremophiles. Antarctic extremophiles have adapted to the cold. They have also adapted to lack of sunlight and nutrients. **Methanogens** are microscopic organisms found at the bottom of Antarctica's Ace Lake. The water there is near freezing and has no oxygen.

Leopard seals are only found on the coast of Antarctica, mainly around the Antarctic Peninsula.

The Antarctic Peninsula is the northernmost part of Antarctica. It is 1,200 miles (2,000 km) long. Its monthly temperatures range from a high of 33° Fahrenheit to a low of 5°F (1° Celsius to –15°C). This peninsula is considered a mountain range. Much of its coastline is covered with ice shelves. These are large, thick sections of ice. There are even some volcanoes on the peninsula's South Shetland Islands.

The majority of Antarctica's animal and plant life can be found on the peninsula. During the warmer seasons, ice melts on the northwest coast. Other coastal areas become ice-free during warmer seasons. They include sections of southern Victoria Land, Wilkes Land, and parts of Ross Island on McMurdo Sound.

Antarctic Peninsula

Peninsula

Antarctica

The average temperature has been increasing by almost 1 degree Fahrenheit (0.55 degree Celsius) per decade since the late 1940s.

The peninsula receives **almost 20 inches** **(50 centimeters)** of precipitation per year, mostly in the form of rain.

A female Antarctic fur seal can live up to 23 years.

More than 30 million crabeater seals live on Antarctica's coasts.

Some summer days have 24 hours of sunlight.

An estimated 8 million pairs of chinstrap penguins live on the Antarctic Peninsula.

Where in the World?

Antarctica covers almost 20 percent of the Southern Hemisphere. This continent lies mostly within the Antarctic Circle, which is located at the 66°30' south latitude.

The South Pole is located roughly in the middle of the continent. It is the southernmost point on Earth. Average temperatures at the South Pole range from –6°F (–21°C) in the summer to –101°F (–78°C) in the winter. Most **precipitation** on Antarctica occurs in the form of snow. High winds in the coldest of areas blow most moisture away. Very few things can live in these cold dry spots.

ATLANTIC OCEAN
AFRICA
MADAGASCAR
SOUTH AMERICA
SOUTHERN OCEAN
INDIAN OCEAN
ANTARTICA
SOUTHERN OCEAN
PACIFIC OCEAN
SOUTHERN OCEAN
TASMANIA
AUSTRALIA

Antarctica experiences seasons opposite to those in the Northern Hemisphere. Its winter occurs in the months of June, July, and August. At this time, Earth's axis tilts the Southern Hemisphere away from the Sun. As a result, Antarctica is in darkness for two weeks around June 21. In the summer, the Southern Hemisphere is tilted toward the Sun, and the continent has two weeks when the Sun never sets.

Antarctic Biomes

A biome is an environment that has a unique climate as well as plants and animals that grow and live there. A continent can have several different biomes within it. Antarctica has three distinct land biomes. They are arctic **tundra**, ice caps, and desert.

Russia's Vostok Research Station is located at the center of the East Antarctica ice sheet. In 1983, it recorded the coldest temperature ever measured on Earth, −128.6°F (−89.2°C).

Antarctica Biome Map

SOUTHERN
OCEAN

SOUTHERN
OCEAN

A N T A R C T I C A

SOUTHERN
OCEAN

Legend

- Arctic Tundra
- Ice Sheet
- Desert
- Land
- Ocean

0   1000 Miles

0   1000 Kilometers

Antarctic Land Biomes

Each of Antarctica's land biomes shares similar characteristics. They are all very cold. They are also very dry. This continent receives less than 8 inches (20.3 cm) of precipitation along its coast each year.

Antarctica shares similar biomes to the Arctic region around the North Pole. The closer the biome is to the South Pole, the fewer life-forms are found. Warmer biomes can support more diverse life.

Arctic Tundra

The Antarctic Peninsula and its neighboring islands are classified as arctic tundra. This region has the most abundant life forms.

Plants: The ground cover is made up of various mosses and lichens. Two of Antarctica's only flowering plants, the Antarctic hair grass and the Antarctic pearlwort, grow here.

Animals: Penguins and seals can be found along the peninsula. The leopard seal is one of the few predators that hunt Antarctica's penguins.

Winter
14°F to −13°F
(−10°C to −25°C)

Summer
32°F to 59°F
(0°C to 15°C)

Precipitation
4 to 6"
(10 to 15 cm) annually

Ice Caps

The Antarctic ice cap biome is located around the South Pole region. The ice is called **permafrost** because it never melts. Permafrost makes up the center of the Antarctic ice sheet. Very few life forms can survive the extreme conditions in the permafrost area.

Plants: Near the South Pole, scientists have found some species of moss and lichen.

Animals: No native life forms have been found at the location of the South Pole. Mites, as well as small flies called midges, live in nearby regions.

Year Round Temperatures −4°F to −76°F (−20° to −60°C)

 Precipitation 2 to 4" (5 to 10 cm) **per year**

Desert

Found near the McMurdo Sound, the McMurdo Dry Valleys consist of three parallel valleys. The Victoria, Wright, and Taylor Valleys are some of the world's most extreme deserts.

Plants: The frozen deserts of Antarctica have the least diverse plant life on Earth. Scientists have discovered microscopic algae, fungi, and bacteria that live inside rocks. There are also blue-green algae that grow at the bottom of lakes.

Animals: The desert is home to a tiny creature called the Antarctic nematode. This microscopic worm feeds on bacteria in the frozen soil.

Winter −20° to −22°F (−29° to −30°C)
Summer 28° to 39°F (−2° to 4°C)

 Precipitation 0.12 to 1.97" (0.3 to 5 cm) **annually**

Antarctic Ecosystems and Habitats

A ntarctica has several unique habitats and ecosystems within its biomes. An ecosystem is made up of organisms such as plants and animals. These organisms rely on one another and their environment for food and shelter.

An ecosystem is made up of habitats. A habitat defines where a specific species of plant or animal lives. A habitat is home to an organism and provides everything it needs to live, including food, water, oxygen, and a survivable temperature.

Most habitats are found in the ice-free regions of Antarctica. These regions can be found both inland and along the coast. Antarctica's coastal habitats are inhabited by large populations of birds and seals. Communities of algae, fungi, and lichens are found in the continent's inland ice-free areas.

Ice shelves make up nearly half of Antarctica's coastline.

In the McMurdo Dry Valleys, organisms are adapted for some of the most extreme conditions on Earth. The average temperature never rises above 23°F (−5°C). Fungi, algae, and bacteria have been found inside rocks. These life forms live off the minerals found in the rocks. Worm-like nematodes feed off the algae.

A very unusual ecosystem exists at Blood Falls, near the Taylor Glacier. Microscopic bacteria live hundreds of feet (m) under the glacier, where there is no sunlight. The bacteria react chemically with elements in the water to produce nutrients. This process is called **chemosynthesis**.

The McMurdo Dry Valleys are one of the largest ice-free regions on Antarctica.

Plant Life in Antarctica

Antarctica was once thought of as virtually a lifeless habitat. The extreme cold and dry conditions made it very difficult for any plants to grow. In the 1970s, scientists discovered microscopic algae and bacteria clinging to cracks between rocks. They are able to survive on very little water and sunlight. Many algae species adapted to being frozen and thawed repeatedly. Most vegetation is found along the warmer coastline of Antarctica. Other areas, such as the McMurdo Dry Valleys, contain plants that are adapted to live in a frozen desert.

The smell of crushed red algae is similar to the scent of watermelon.

Red Algae

Red algae can be found on snow slopes throughout Antarctica. In the spring, snow on top of glaciers begins to melt. Algae form in the running streams. They absorb nutrients from the liquid water. The algae develop a red protective chemical that shields them from the energy of the Sun.

Buellia Frigida

Buellia frigida is one of the most abundant endemic species on Antarctica. These blackish gray plants are found in the northern and coastal regions and look like splattered paint on the rocks. They get their nutrients from bird droppings. The average size for this lichen is about 6 inches (15 cm) in diameter.

Buellia frigida can be found at all elevations, from sea level to mountainous regions.

Antarctic Pearlwort

Antarctic pearlwort is one of only two flowering plants on Antarctica. It is found on the South Orkney Islands, South Shetland Islands, and on the western and northern coasts of the Antarctic Peninsula. This plant grows, blooms, and creates seeds during the very short summer season. It then lies **dormant** for the winter. The Antarctic pearlwort holds moisture because it has small leaves.

Small plants like the Antarctic pearlwort have developed shallow root systems so they can grow on thin soil layers.

Antarctic Hair Grass

Antarctic hair grass grows in small, yellow-green clumps that look like spiky hair. It is found along the sides of cliffs and in rocky crevices throughout the maritime islands and the Antarctic Peninsula. This hardy plant contains **proteins** that prevent it from freezing. It also makes extra **carbohydrates** for food when the cold sets in. Hair grass is **self-fertilizing**. It does not always have to rely on **pollination** to reproduce. Small tufts may break away from the plant and re-grow elsewhere if carried by birds or the wind.

Antarctic hair grass has a wax coating on its leaves. This keeps moisture from evaporating.

Just the Facts

Antarctica has more than 200 species of lichens.

Antarctic hair grass has thrived in extreme Antarctic conditions for more than 12,000 years.

More than **300** *species of algae are found in Antarctica.*

Some species of algae will grow as little as 0.39 inches (1 cm) every 1,000 years.

Insects and Insect-like Creatures

Antarctica has far fewer life forms than other continents. There is really only one true insect species on the continent. Insects belong to a larger group of organisms called arthropods, which include Antarctica's other insect-like organisms. Arthropods are an important part of Antarctica's various ecosystems. They provide food for other animals and churn up soil, which allows plants to grow. Some arthropods that live in Antarctica are **parasites**. They rely on other creatures to survive, often harming them in the process. Ticks belong to a group of parasites that live in the fur and feathers of other animals. They bite and feed on the blood of the animal that protects them from the harsh wind and cold.

Mites have been found closer to the South Pole than any other arthropod.

Mites

Mites are members of the arthropod family. Antarctic mites live in soil and rock crevices and are able to survive the extreme cold by a process called "supercooling." They survive the cold by producing an "anti-freeze" chemical, which keeps the liquid in their bodies from freezing.

Collembola

Collembola are also known as springtails. These six-legged creatures live under rocks along the coast. They eat fungi and algae. To survive the extreme cold, they slow down their body functions to conserve energy. Collembola are also adapted to survive extreme cold by supercooling.

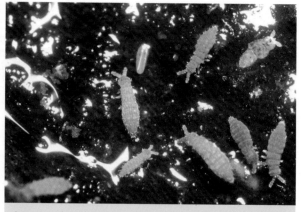

At just under 0.04 inches (1 mm) long, the collembola is one of Antarctica's largest land animals.

Tardigrades

Tardigrades are microscopic animals found in the most extreme ecosystems of the Antarctic. They eat algae and make their way through ice and frozen soil using claws on their eight legs. Though tardigrades live in moist habitats, along with mosses and lichens, they can survive very long dry periods in a "freeze-dried" state.

Tardigrades are sometimes called water bears.

Nematodes

Nematodes are small arthropods that look like worms. These burrowing creatures are widely distributed throughout the soils of McMurdo Dry Valleys. Their diet consists of bacteria. Like other Antarctic arthropods, nematodes are also adapted for supercooling.

The nematode is Antarctica's most numerous land animal.

Just the Facts

Antarctica has about 67 recorded species of insects.

The Belgica antarctica, a type of midge, is Antarctica's largest land animal. It is only about 1/3-inch (0.8 cm) long.

Earthworms, spiders, beetles, and flies live in the warmer climates of the islands off the mainland.

Most Antarctic insects are less than 0.08 inch (2 mm) long.

The Parochlus steineni, another type of midge, is the only winged insect living on Antarctica.

Birds and Mammals

Antarctica has no endemic mammal species. Conditions are far too cold for most mammals. The only mammal that ever makes its way onto Antarctica is the seal. Six seal species are found on Antarctica and its islands. They include the southern elephant seal, the southern fur seal, the Weddell seal, and the Ross seal. There are also six species of penguin native to Antarctica. Both penguins and seals feed on the abundant sea life that exists in Antarctica's marine ecosystem.

Emperor Penguin

The emperor penguin is the largest penguin species in the world. It feeds on fish and krill and can grow to a height of 45 inches (115 cm). Emperor penguins keep warm by huddling in groups. Females lay a single egg, and then male penguins keep the eggs warm and safe. Females return to care for their young. Eventually, the chicks will enter the water and begin hunting for food.

Emperor penguins lay their eggs in May and June. The eggs hatch about 70 days later. By December, the chicks will have grown their adult feathers.

Snow Petrel

The snow petrel is about the size of a pigeon and is one of the few bird species that breeds exclusively in Antarctica. Petrels nest farther into the interior of the continent than any other bird. They have even been spotted at the South Pole. Petrels feed on fish, krill and other small marine animals. They will also eat the carcasses of dead seals and birds.

Snow petrels are often spotted on Antarctica's many icebergs.

Leopard Seal

The leopard seal is an aggressive predator. It can grow up to 9 feet (3 m) in length and weigh up to 882 pounds (400 kg). The name "leopard" comes from the seal's spotted fur. Long sharp teeth allow these seals to hunt fish, penguins, and other aquatic birds.

Leopard seals are very powerful swimmers. They can pop out of the water to surprise and capture penguins on the ice surface.

The Blue-Eyed Shag

Blue-eyed shags belong to a class of birds called cormorants. They rarely venture very far from land. Shags nest year round on the rocks of the western side of the Antarctic Peninsula. They work together in groups to fish. They float together by the hundreds, each taking a turn diving for fish. Like penguins, shags can dive to depths of more than 400 feet (122 m). They are often caught and eaten by seals.

The blue-eyed shag does not have blue eyes, but rather a ring of blue skin that circles its eyes.

Just the Facts

Of the **350 million** birds living in the Antarctic, about 1/2 are penguins.

An estimated **4 million** snow petrels live in Antarctica.

The Weddell seal can hold its breath underwater for up to **80 minutes.**

The southern elephant seal can weigh up to 8,800 pounds (4,000 kg).

Antarctic Aquatic Biomes

The majority of Antarctica's wildlife is found along its 11,165 miles (17,968 km) of coastline. The aquatic biome plays an important part in sustaining much of this life. The marine biome includes the salt water of the ocean. The freshwater biome includes the lakes, rivers, and streams on the continent.

Marine Biome

Antarctica is surrounded by the Southern Ocean. This is the fourth largest ocean in the world. The ecosystems in this marine biome are defined by the depth of the water and its temperature. Water that is closer to the surface is warmer because it is exposed to the Sun. Different plants and animals can live at different depths depending on the temperature.

Plants: Plants growing in Antarctica's marine biome include phytoplankton, algae, and seaweed.
Animals: Krill, whales, fish, and seals are the main animals living in the waters around Antarctica.

About 3% salt content

Aquatic Ecosystems and Habitats

There are many freshwater ecosystems and habitats throughout the continent of Antarctica. Many subglacial lakes support ecosystems. Lake Vostok, located near the South Pole, is covered in ice that is 2.49 miles (4 km) thick. Scientists believe the flowing water below the ice sustains microscopic life. Ice streams form due to the pressure from glaciers. The flowing water provides a habitat for algae to grow. Ice streams also help glaciers flow to the sea.

Algae can be seen growing in the waters of Green Creek, a glacial meltwater stream in Antarctica's Victoria Land.

Freshwater Biome

The Antarctic ice sheet contains almost 70 percent of all the freshwater on Earth. Glacial melt in the spring creates ice streams and rivers. These rivers feed many of the lakes in the region. Many of Antarctica's lakes have water underneath the ice. There are several frozen lakes in the McMurdo Dry Valley.

Plants: Several types of algae can be found in Antarctica's freshwater lakes and rivers.
Other Organisms: Microscopic bacteria and microbes can also be found living in Antarctica's freshwater biome.

Less than 1% salt content

Antarctic Aquatic Life

The ocean surrounding Antarctica is an important part of a system that moves water around the globe. Antarctica's cold ocean water is much more dense than the warmer waters to its north. Cold water sinks to the ocean floor, causing warmer water to rise. This motion helps circulate the water in Earth's oceans, which creates a unique ecosystem in Antarctica's marine biome.

The Antarctic krill is the most abundant krill species in the world.

Krill

Tiny shrimp-like krill are an important food source for Antarctica's sea animals. Many creatures, from sea-birds to blue whales, depend on krill for food. On average, a krill is 2.4 inches (6 cm) in length and weighs less than one tenth of an ounce (3 g). Krill feed on microscopic plants. Some scientists consider krill to be the most important animals in Antarctica's marine biome.

Antarctic Cod

The Antarctic cod can grow to a length of 4.92 feet (1.5 m) and a weight of 55 pounds (25 kg). It only lives in the Southern Ocean and has adapted to cold water. The cod's blood has anti-freeze proteins in it. This allows the cod to swim in cold waters without freezing.

The Antarctic cod is generally found in the Ross Sea area of the Southern Ocean.

Blue Whale

Blue whales are the largest animals on Earth, reaching lengths of 89 feet (27 m) and weighing up to 200 tons (181 metric tons). They visit the Antarctic region during the summer months. During that time, they will feed almost nonstop for up to 8 months. Their main food source is krill. In one day, a blue whale can consume 6 tons (5.4 t) of krill.

Blue whales filter krill through baleen plates in their mouths.

Icefish

Icefish are found near the coastlines of Antarctica. They are the only fish without red blood cells, so their blood is colorless. In other animals, red blood cells transport oxygen throughout the body. Fortunately, icefish can absorb oxygen through the skin. These fish can only live in extremely cold, oxygen-rich waters. Warmer waters have less oxygen, and icefish could not absorb enough to survive.

Icefish can survive in water that ranges in temperature from 28°F to 39°F (−2 to 4°C).

The Antarctic cod lives at depths up to **5,000 feet** (1,524 m) below the ocean surface.

One adult blue whale weighs as much as 25 African elephants.

16 different species of icefish are found in the waters around **Antarctica**.

6 billion tons (5.4 billion metric tons) of krill are found throughout the Southern Ocean.

Maintaining Balance

Antarctica's various habitats are all similar, especially in terms of temperature. Antarctica's life forms have adapted to the cold environment. Plants have learned to live with little water. Animals that feed off these plants have adapted to the challenge of finding nutrients in them. There is a delicate balance that must be maintained in nature. All levels of life rely on one another in a balanced ecosystem. Small changes in the ecosystem can affect the entire continent.

Ozone Hole

The ozone layer protects Earth's atmosphere from the harmful rays of the Sun. This protective layer is particularly thin at the South Pole. The size of the hole varies. In 2013, its maximum size was 9.3 million square miles (24.0 million sq. km). Scientists say the ultraviolet (UV) light that passes through the hole in the ozone layer harms icefish. Antarctic marine plants are also affected by the hole in the ozone. This UV damage starts a chain reaction that can eventually affect the entire ecosystem.

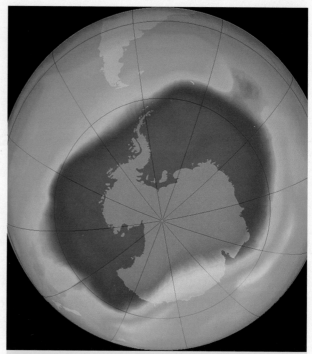

In 2006, a NASA satellite showed that the average area of Antarctic ozone hole was 10.6 million square miles (27.5 million sq. km). That is the largest ozone hole on record.

Human Interaction

Almost 40,000 people visited Antarctica in 2010. Officials work to reduce the impact the tourism industry has on the region. There are restrictions on the number of people able to visit at one time. They are also looking to reduce pollution caused by tour ships.

Ecosystem Interactions

All organisms in an ecosystem interact with each other. They are each part of a food chain. Every food chain contains producers, primary and secondary consumers, and decomposers. Producers are plants that use the Sun's energy to make food. Primary consumers are herbivores that eat plants. Secondary consumers feed on the herbivores. Decomposers break down dead organisms and return nutrients to the soil.

Penguins
Penguins are secondary consumers. Their diet is made up mainly of krill and fish.

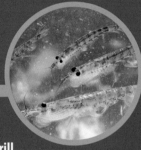

Krill
Krill are primary consumers. They eat phytoplankton. Krill is a primary food source for many marine consumers from small fish to enormous blue whales.

Leopard Seal
Leopard seals are one of hundreds of secondary consumers that eat krill. Leopard seals also eat several other secondary consumers like penguins, fish, and sea birds.

Bacteria
Bacteria are decomposers. They break down dead matter, such as the carcasses of krill, seals and other animals in the ocean.

Phytoplankton
Phytoplankton are microscopic organisms. They are producers that create food through photosynthesis. Phytoplankton is a main food source for the tiny krill.

Diversity for Humans

Antarctica plays a key role in Earth's heat balance. Heat from the Sun is absorbed by Earth's atmosphere and is then reflected back into space. As ice is more reflective than water and land, Antarctica's ice sheet is better able to reflect heat away from Earth's surface. This keeps the planet from overheating. When this ice sheet shrinks, more solar radiation stays in Earth's atmosphere. This contributes to **global warming.**

Scientists have found blue-green algae at the bottom of some of Antarctica's lakes. They are believed to be some of Earth's earliest life forms. They may also have been the original sources of oxygen on Earth.

Human Impact

One of the biggest threats to Antarctica is world pollution. The buildup of greenhouse gases from fuel use contributes to global warming. Studies show that global warming has affected the melting of Antarctica's ice shelves. From 1992 to 2011, West Antarctica and the Antarctic Peninsula lost a combined 187,392 billion pounds (85 billion t) of ice a year. This has created a loss of habitat for animals such as seals and penguins.

Scientists take core samples from ice walls to gauge how Antarctica's climate has changed over time.

No matter the size, motored boats pollute both the air and water around Antarctica. They and their passengers have the potential to cause serious environmental damage to the area.

Conserving Nature

Scientists, governments, and nature groups are working hard to conserve Antarctica's delicate ecosystems. In 1978, the United States passed the Antarctic Conservation Act. It outlined strict rules for scientific study in Antarctica. This included protection of plants and animals and antipollution laws.

The Antarctic Treaty, signed by 50 countries, has designated dozens of protected areas on the continent and in several ocean regions. Animal and plant life in these areas are protected by rules and regulations enforced by the treaty. Plants and animals cannot be removed from these areas. New plants and animals cannot be introduced to these areas. Some life forms have even been designated as specially protected species.

The United States operates three research stations. At McMurdo Station, located 850 miles (1,368 km) north of the South Pole, scientific studies include research into the effects of climate change on permafrost.

Make an Ecosystem Web

Use this book and research on the Internet, to create an Antarctic ecosystem.

1. Find an Antarctic plant or animal. Think about what habitat it lives in.
2. Find at least three organisms that are found in the same habitat. This could include plants, insects, birds and mammals.
3. How do these species interact with each other? Do they provide food or shelter for the other organisms?
4. Begin linking these organisms together to show which organisms rely on each other for food or shelter.
5. Once your ecosystem web is complete, think about how removing one organism would affect the other organisms in the web.

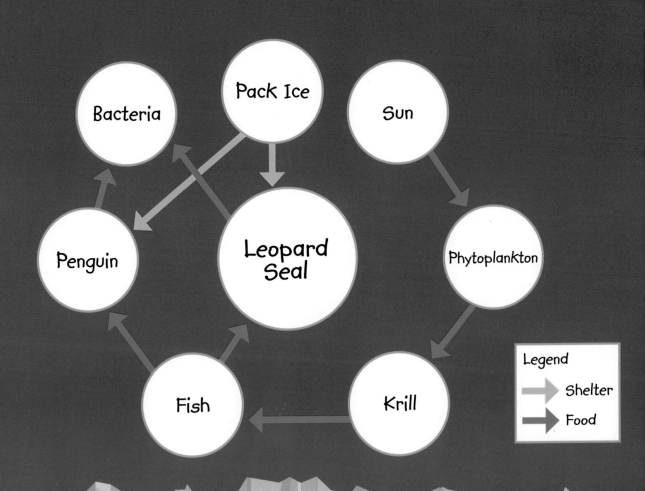

Quiz

1 How much of Antarctica is covered by the Antarctic ice sheet?

5.29 million sq. miles (13.72 million sq. km)

2 How many species of penguin can be found on Antarctica?

9

3 What percentage of Antarctica is barren rock?

2 percent

6 What kind of biome is the classification for the Antarctic Peninsula?

Arctic tundra

7 What is one of the biggest threats to Antarctica?

Pollution

4 What are the names of Antarctica's two flowering plants?

Antarctic hair grass and Antarctic pearlwort

5 What is the average winter temperature at the South Pole?

−101°F (−74°C)

9 What is the largest penguin species in the world?

Emperor penguin

8 What is Antarctica's most plentiful land animal?

Nematodes

10 How much of Earth's freshwater is contained in the Antarctic ice sheet?

Nearly 70 percent

Key Words

carbohydrates: a class of nutrients that includes sugars and starches

chemosynthesis: a process in which organisms generate energy

dormant: when normal physical functions stop for a period of time

endemic: something found in only one area of the world

global warming: the gradual warming of Earth believed to be caused by pollution and greenhouse gases

methanogens: bacteria producing a gas called methane

parasites: organisms that live in or on other organisms and rely on them for food

permafrost: a layer of soil that remains frozen throughout the year

pollination: the fertilization process for a plant

precipitation: any form of moisture such as snow or rain

proteins: a class of nutrient that is essential to all living things

self-fertilizing: plants that can fertilize themselves without help from other animals

species: a group of organisms that are similar and can produce offspring

tundra: a vast and treeless region characterized by cold climate

Index

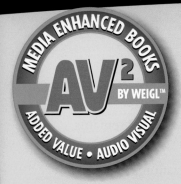

Log on to www.av2books.com

AV² by Weigl brings you media enhanced books that support active learning. Go to www.av2books.com, and enter the special code found on page 2 of this book. You will gain access to enriched and enhanced content that supplements and complements this book. Content includes video, audio, weblinks, quizzes, a slide show, and activities.

AV² Online Navigation

Audio
Listen to sections of the book read aloud.

Book Pages
AV² pages directly correspond to pages in the book.

Video
Watch informative video clips.

Key Words
Study vocabulary, and complete a matching word activity.

Embedded Weblinks
Gain additional information for research.

Try This!
Complete activities and hands-on experiments.

Quizzes
Test your knowledge.

Slide Show
View images and captions, and prepare a presentation.

AV² was built to bridge the gap between print and digital. We encourage you to tell us what you like and what you want to see in the future.

Sign up to be an AV² Ambassador at www.av2books.com/ambassador.